The
Divorce
Resource
Series

Why Me?

A Teen Guide to Divorce and Your Feelings

Rachel Aydt

THE ROSEN PUBLISHING GROUP, INC. NEW YORK

This book could clearly be dedicated to only one person:
Mama, I love you to the moon and back.

Published in 2000 by The Rosen Publishing Group, Inc.
29 East 21st Street, New York, NY 10010

First Edition

Library of Congress Cataloging-in-Publication Data

Aydt, Rachel.
    Why me?: a teen guide to divorce and your feelings/ Rachel Aydt.
        p. cm— (The divorce resource series)
    Includes bibliographical references and index.
    Summary: Offers advice on the emotional aspects of divorce for teenagers whose parents are divorcing.
    ISBN 0-8239-3113-7
    1. Children of divorced parents— United States— Psychology— Juvenile literature. 2. Teenagers— United States— Psychology— Juvenile literature.   3. Teenagers— United States— Life skills guides— juvenile literature. [1. Divorce.] I. Title. II. Series.

HQ777.5.A94 1999
306.89—dc21   99-048528

Manufactured in the United States of America

Contents

Introduction

If your parents are splitting up, it may feel like the most earth-shattering thing in the world. You may be going through lots of changes: a new home, new school, even a new family. You might need to pitch in a lot more around the house, get a part-time job, or even appear in family court.

At the same time, you may feel as if you have no one to turn to. It is very easy during this time for parents to be only focused on their own feelings, and you may have a hard time telling them how *you* feel. You may not feel comfortable confiding in your friends. As a result, you can end up feeling confused and totally alone.

A divorce can be devastating.

So, how can you cope with your feelings right now? It's hard enough to handle what comes up in life when everything is normal. So where will the extra energy come from that you will need to console your parents? Siblings? Yourself? How will you deal with moving back and forth between two households? Why do you feel responsible for having to make everything better? Why do you feel responsible that everything fell apart to begin with? What happens when you can't deal with your stepparents or stepsiblings?

Whatever your situation is, this book will offer some advice on how to maneuver your way through this difficult time. Believe it or not, all of these feelings are normal, and you have more power over your feelings than you might think. And even though you may feel alone, you aren't! In this book you'll find out how to find people who will support you.

Your opinions and emotions about your parents' divorce are important. By learning how to express them, confide them in others, and work them out, the experience of divorce may not be all bad. Instead, it can be an incredible time of growth and independence for you.

CHAPTER 1

Tension at Home

It was really weird how my parents started fighting like crazy. It started with small stuff, like my mom crying a lot and saying how Dad didn't help out with anything, how tired she was, things like that. Then it seemed to get worse, as if nothing he could do was right, which didn't really seem fair to me. Brian, my little brother, and I would try to stay out of the house, but after a while the noise seemed inescapable. — Maria

Maria's situation is pretty common. It's not always easy to understand why parents fight. After all, it makes them feel terrible. But what's even worse is how it can make you feel—and you're not even the one in

Common Problems

There are common problems in families that cause a lot of stress. Perhaps there are too many bills to pay, and the money's getting tight. Another common problem in families is alcoholism and drug abuse. If one of your parents has a problem, you are not alone. There are groups that you could get involved with that would help you out a lot if your parents suffer from alcohol or drug problems, such as Al-Anon. (See the Where to Go for Help section at the back of this book.) These groups are confidential and can help you by introducing you to other people who are going through the same thing.

If there is any physical abuse going on in your house, you need to ask for help. One good person to speak with is your school counselor, who is trained to treat your problems with confidentiality, and who can tell you who to contact in your community.

the fight! So what are you supposed to do when things get loud, angry, and scary at home?

Chances are, a lot of smaller struggles between your parents have been mounting, and this is just the way the pent-up anger shows itself. It won't last forever, and it's important during this time to try to be as clear about your own feelings as possible—not just to your parents, but to yourself.

It may be uneasy adjusting to a new family life when one parent leaves.

Starting to Sort It Out

It is difficult to figure out why your parents are at each other's throats all the time. And although the conflicts between your parents may run deep, tempers will often flare up over little things.

Isolating a few of the sources of your parents' fights might make them seem smaller and more manageable to you. Remember that old phrase, "You're making a mountain out of a molehill"? Looking at each of the molehills individually can give you some perspective. Instead of saying, "My parents are in another huge and nasty fight," you can say to yourself, "Who cares that Dad dropped the plate? Big deal." Although you can't change the fact that they're not getting along, you can help put things in perspective.

Those Dreaded Words: "We're Getting a Divorce"

One morning my mom and dad sat down with me and my little brother because they said they had something important to tell us. They were both really serious, and I was really worried about what they were going to say. My mom started by saying, "First of all, Daddy and I want you to know that we love you both very much." I don't know why, but this made me sad and I started to cry. Then Dad said, "Your mom and I have decided that even though we still love each other, we can't live together anymore. We're getting a divorce." — Wendy

For Wendy, this news hit her hard, as if someone had dropped a bomb. Her stomach felt twisted, and her heart felt like it jumped in her throat. At first she felt stunned, and then she felt sad. These feelings were also mixed in with fear, confusion, and uncertainty. She became increasingly nervous about how things were going to be in the future for her and her little brother.

When your parents first tell you that they're getting divorced, it feels like your world is caving in around you. There is no doubt that this is going be a challenging and difficult time, but with a little guidance and thought, you can make it better. There are people you can talk to, groups you can join, books you can read, as well as many other resources you can go to for help.

Just about everybody has a friend whose parents have divorced. Maybe the friend was so young that he or she doesn't even remember going through it; maybe your friend spends summers somewhere exotic with the other parent; maybe he or she does not see the other parent at all.

No matter how a friend's situation turned out, remember that your situation is unique. Just because one friend's father split town and she doesn't see him anymore does not mean that the same thing is going to happen to your family. Keep your cool and remember that for a little while, there will be some changes. You can get through it if you give yourself a break and take things one step at a time.

CHAPTER 2

The Transition After the News

When most people think of divorce, their minds fill up with negative terms: *anger*, *sadness*, and *confusion*. Although these terms definitely apply to what you are going through, they focus only on the negative aspects. Believe it or not, there is a positive side to divorce. It just takes a bit of time to get through the painful side of the process before we can understand its benefits. Imagine hearing the word *divorce* and having these positive words come to mind: *change, relief, expansion, learning, growth,* and *strength.*

You are feeling the effects of one of the most common shake-ups that the American family experiences.

Fifty percent of American marriages end in divorce! Whenever you feel overwhelmed or ashamed about your parents' divorce, remember that you are not a freak who is living through something so horrible, bizarre, and upsetting that no one else can relate to your situation. More people than you can imagine have already lived through this.

Some Common Questions

For every kid who is uncomfortable at home because his or her parents fight, there is another who has lived through it. You are not the only one who feels compelled to hide out in your room permanently or go live with a friend for a while. It might be helpful for you to know some common questions that kids and teenagers have when their parents fight.

Do my parents fight because of me?

You might feel as if your parents are fighting because of you—something you did (or didn't do) or even the fact that you're *there*. It is important to remember that if you come up in their arguments, it's not your fault that they can't get along. Your parents love you no matter what they are fighting about.

> You may feel as if your parents divorce is your fault even though it is not.

How come it seems as though my parents suddenly hate each other?

Often adults argue over smaller things that suddenly build up. Or they may have been trying to work their problems out together privately for a long time, but ultimately they aren't able to reconcile. They may feel bitter, or feel as if they failed. Whatever the reason, when things are tense sometimes the smallest incident will set off an explosion.

This may have happened to you. Just think of a time when you got into a fight with a friend of yours and couldn't figure out why. Even if your friend Mary got another A on her math test, and you got a B even though you and Mary studied together, it still doesn't make sense that you would flare up over something so minor. But maybe last week Mary said something mean to you in front of other friends, and you haven't forgotten it.

Just remember that it's probably better for your parents to show their feelings instead of keeping them all in. You might have hated fighting with Mary, but chances are you felt better when it was over. For many people, fighting is the most immediate way to get a resolution.

What can I do?

You may feel inclined to disappear if your parents are fighting all the time. Sometimes it's appropriate to go to your room or to go visit a friend for some relief. But when things quiet down again, it's important and mature for you to tell your parents how it makes you feel when they fight. It's good for them to hear that you get angry and upset when they yell at each other. Your parents care about how you feel, and so it could be helpful for them to hear you express yourself right now.

It's not your fault that your parents are arguing a lot, and it's not your job to keep the peace. *They're the grownups.*

How do I stay out of the middle?

The best way to stay out the middle of your parents' arguments is to steer clear of them. You might find that when your mom isn't around, your dad starts bad-mouthing her to you, or vice versa. It might feel good for that parent to blow off some more steam, but if you can't stand hearing it anymore, tell your parent that you don't want to be in the middle. If he or she gets mad at you, just remember that it is temporary. Your parents might be mad at themselves and embarrassed about trying to get you involved. They'll get over it. Even if you have to repeat yourself a few times and ask them to keep you out of the middle, they should eventually respond to your feelings.

Why am I taking sides?

Even though you aren't the one fighting right now, it doesn't mean that you don't hear what your parents are fighting about. You are a member of the family and the household, and you will certainly have an opinion about what's being hashed out. Chances are, that opinion will sway in favor of one parent.

Empathizing with one parent is normal right now, and you shouldn't feel guilty for doing so. This doesn't mean that you don't love your other parent; you might just be on the same wavelength as your mom or your dad right now.

It's not your fault

Someone must have written a rule that goes like this: Every kid whose parents are getting divorced will feel guilty for one reason or another. To get through this tough time with some reasonable expectations of yourself, you'll have to get over the guilt . . . fast! Here are a few examples of other people's guilt, and responses explaining why their parents' divorce was not their fault.

My parents got divorced because of money. I think I have a lot to do with this, since I'm just another mouth to feed. — John

Your parents decided to have you. But if they are divorcing, the problems they are having are between the two of them. No child is the cause of his or her parents' divorce, even if the parents are quarreling over the child.

I think my parents had more fun until I came along. After I was born, my mom had to put more focus on me, and less on my dad. I think that's why they're getting a divorce. — Maria

It's not your fault that your parents don't fit well together anymore. Besides—whatever it is that broke them apart had nothing to do with how much they love you.

Why can't I figure out how to make my parents like each other again? It's as though they don't even know each other anymore. — Hakim

People change. Some marriages can weather the changes that people experience, but other times it's natural for people to grow apart. This is why most people get divorced to begin with.

My parents feel like failures because they're getting a divorce, and no matter how much I try to tell myself that it doesn't have anything to do with me, it's hard. They fight a lot, and a lot of the time they're fighting over what to do with me. — Robin

Your parents are not failures. Half of all marriages end in divorce! If you feel as if they're fighting because of you, remember that their arguments are a symptom of deeper problems between the two of them. In other words, they would find something to argue about even if you were not around.

CHAPTER 3

When Someone Moves Out

When my mom said that she was moving out, I was shocked. I couldn't imagine life without my mom right there. What if she decided to move far away? Would she be around to see me graduate from high school? I didn't know if I had a choice to go with her or not. The whole thing was very scary at first. — Tom

Custody: What It Means

Custody establishes which parent a child or children will live with after a divorce. Some parents divide custody, which means that children divide their time between two households. This arrangement is known as joint custody. Other parents set up various systems in which children alternate homes from week to week.

How a family decides to handle custody depends on multiple factors that are unique to each family. The options are many. Sometimes custody starts out one way and ends up another. Usually when parents divorce, children end up spending more time with one parent than another.

The Custody Battle and Family Court

You might be in for a bumpy ride if your parents disagree about whom you will live with after the divorce. This disagreement is sometimes referred to as a custody battle. Who retains custody is normally determined in family court. Family court is the sector of the judicial system that settles such matters.

You may be brought to court to testify in front of a judge about your own custodial issues. If you are, the questions might be difficult and awkward for you to answer openly, since both parents might be seated in the courtroom. This is an extreme example of the tug-of-war that can happen between parents and their children during a divorce. Both parents will hire lawyers and present their sides of the story to a judge. Their lawyers will be very sympathetic with your awkward position, and they might even interview you in private. Rest assured, the family court has your best interest in mind when it makes its custody decision. You are absolutely its top priority.

Who Moves?

If It's You . . .

When parents divorce, the transition can be a complicated one. New routines take time to be established. This includes someone moving out. It's tough to face the reality that soon you won't be living with one of your parents.

Of course, the easiest possible transition that could occur is that you will simply stay in the house or apartment where you are living now. However, you may have to move into a new place. If this is the case, the changes are coming so fast and furious that they are probably overwhelming you. The first thing that might change immediately is your school, which is an enormous adjustment. You might not be living as close to your neighborhood friends anymore, which is unsettling. Although it's crucial that you make every effort to adjust to your new school, it's also important to keep in touch with your old friends. Let your parents know that doing so will make things a lot easier on you. You need to have opportunities to hang out with your old friends, if possible.

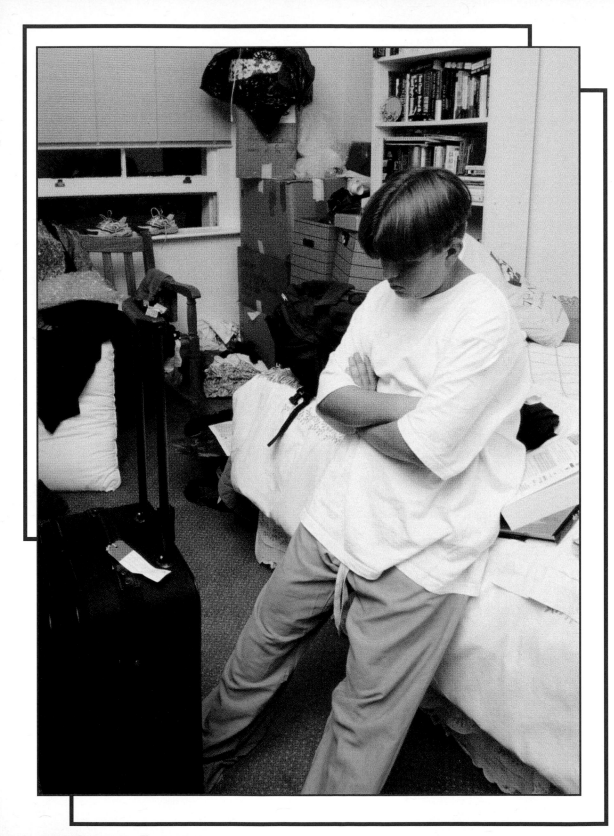

If you are changing schools, be sure to introduce yourself to your new school counselor. He or she will be more than happy to show you around and tell you about extracurricular activities that are going on. Don't be afraid to tell him or her why you've switched schools—you're doing yourself a favor by increasing your support network. Your guidance counselor might even be able to point you toward a support group such as Banana Splits (see the Where to Go for Help section at the back of this book), a group that is sponsored by many schools.

If It's Not You . . .

If you continue to live where you were living before your parents' separation, expect to visit your other parent on weekends. This can be an annoying situation, since you're forever packing up stuff and taking it from one place to another.

You will definitely experience temporary inconveniences when someone moves. However, the greatest challenge in this scenario is getting used to the absence of the parent who has moved away. This is a very disruptive and painful change—perhaps the most painful. Before your parents decided to get a divorce, they may have fought a lot, but they were probably both around a lot more. Now you'll have to call your

A change in your regular routine can be really frustrating.

newly absent mom or dad to tell him or her things that might seem small and insignificant. Remember that even the smallest thing you want to talk to your parents about is not insignificant right now. If you feel the need to talk to your parent, it's fine to pick up the phone and call.

It's normal to look back on the bad times with both parents as better than life with the absence of a parent. But you'll breathe easier after your routine shifts and you grow used to the change. No matter how you look at it, there will be less tension in your house than there was.

Over time you will discover that your relationships with your parents might change, even for the better. Your visits with your "absent" parent will probably be for more concentrated blocks of time than you're accustomed to seeing him or her. This might allow your parents to get to know and appreciate your relationship even more than they did before. Shaking things up will force everyone to get more creative about how to spend precious time together.

Changing Relationships

Some parents might be feeling inadequate right now because they aren't used to providing for you by themselves. Maybe your dad played baseball with you, and your mom simply doesn't know how to play. Or maybe it's a lot more complex than that: The parent who moved out is the one who used to listen to all the details of your day. This is a change that may make you feel terribly lonely, and even though this is an old cliche, it holds some truth: Time will heal all wounds—or at least minimize them!

Your Parents' Challenges

Your parents need to be forgiving toward themselves during this major shift and realize that it takes time for new routines to fall into place. You will be a lot better off if you can be forgiving of some of their shortcomings right now.

If your parents separate with a lot of anger, this can make it very difficult for you to feel comfortable with the one who has moved away. A parent might get upset when you come home from a weekend away— he or she might take that frustration out on you. Sadly, this is a very common scenario. Someone could write a whole book on the mistakes that parents make during the transition of divorce. Here are a couple:

The Third Degree

When Rosa and Manuel came home from a weekend away visiting their father, their mother was at home waiting for them, furious. "Where did your father take

you?" "What did you do?" "Does he have a new girl-friend?" "Did he take you to a nice restaurant?" "What are those clothes he sent you home in?" "Does your father think he can buy your love?"

Sound familiar? Sometimes when you go to visit your parent, you come home to an unreasonable line of questioning. This is a very upsetting thing for a parent to do to you, and it's not fair at all.

Even if your parents can't stand each other, they are both still your parents, and it's not your fault they split up! So if you're coming home to this, tell your angry parent that you need to have the freedom to continue your relationship with your mother or father. Even if it makes him or her unhappy, your parent will grow to see that it's better for you in the long run to see both parents.

Delivering Messages

My father was so angry at my mother that he decided he couldn't talk to her on the phone anymore. Whenever he would drive me home from our visits, he would make me pass along information to her instead. "You tell your mother that I'm sick and tired of her calling me and yelling at me all the time." Of course, I wouldn't give my mom mean messages, but it got so annoying! — John

It can be really tough when one parent asks about the other.

Delivering messages between one parent and another is unfair. Perhaps they're so angry that they don't want to talk to each other, or they can't do it without ending up in a screaming match. If you begin to feel that your parents are being unreasonable, speak up. Even if they get mad at you, it's temporary. If you have to repeat yourself, you're still doing the right thing. Eventually they'll hear you and begin communicating with each other.

Your Overwhelmed Parent

If your parent is so upset that he or she takes it out on you, this is completely unfair—but normal. Even though your parent legally has custody and may have even fought in court to keep you with him or her, raising a child and living alone is a major adjustment. In the midst of this adjustment, your parent may say hurtful things he or she doesn't mean. Keep in mind that your parent isn't perfect. Many of the things you are feeling right now, your parents are feeling too. They may be the adults, but from time to time they'll act like children. They might be so sad and overwhelmed that they feel they don't know how to take care of you by themselves.

It takes strength for a parent to care for a child by himself or herself. This strength takes time to build, and in the meantime, you might be exposed to a couple of tantrums. Express how painful these tantrums are for you, and that even though you know they don't mean what they say, it's scary for you to hear. If the tantrums persist after you've expressed how you feel, discuss this with an adult you trust, such as a grandparent or a school counselor.

If you feel overwhelmed, talk to a counselor or trusted adult.

CHAPTER 4

Keeping Your Brain Sane

Sticking Together: You and Your Siblings

It might feel as if your whole life is unraveling right now. Some things are out of your control, like your parents' divorce. Other things are not, like getting along well with your siblings.

When you stop to think about it, siblings are pretty amazing. There is no other kind of relationship in which someone has shared your childhood experiences as intimately as your brothers and/or sisters. Often this includes a lot of fighting—particularly in adolescence, when you are all trying to have your own space.

You and your siblings can be a source of comfort for one another.

The time to stick together is during your parents' separation and divorce. There may be times when you feel like talking about it, but you don't want to discuss it with your friends. Another bonus about getting along well right now is that if you are having to travel back and forth between your parents' homes, you will have an extra buffer of support when times feel lonely. It might take a while to make new friends in the new neighborhood.

If You're an Only Child

If you're an only child, finding support nearby might seem trickier than it does for those who have siblings. Just because you don't have brothers and sisters doesn't mean that you have to feel isolated. You just need to be creative when discovering your support network. Ask yourself these important questions:

Who makes you feel good when you talk with him or her? Who do you tell your problems to? Do you feel close to your grandparents, or do any other relatives or friends of the family live nearby? If you go to church or synagogue, is there a member of the clergy whom you could speak with?

One way to feel some immediate relief from a painful and awkward home life is, simply, to step away from it sometimes. You aren't running away from your problems—you're just giving yourself a break. Answer the previous questions and then seek help from those who make you feel the most comfortable and loved.

Staying Active

After my parents separated, I would get incredibly moody at times. Sometimes I wouldn't even know what was wrong—I was just miserable. After a while I noticed that every time I hiked in the mountains, I felt a lot better. I'm not sure if it was being outside, getting exercise, or being alone, but whatever it was, I decided to keep doing it anytime I felt bad.
— Miguel

Taking long walks can help you to think things through.

Exercise helps to fight depression. If you already participate in after-school sports, you know how much better you feel after running around for a couple of hours. Sports do more than strengthen your body; they strengthen your concentration and temporarily force you to focus only on the game. Extracurricular activities get you away from your house for a little while to hang out with other people your own age.

If you aren't interested in sports, take a good look at the other activities that are offered by your school, local boys and girls clubs, the YMCA . . . even your local library. All are jam-packed with interesting workshops that will broaden your interests, show you a good time, and introduce you to new people.

Explore Your Creativity

Finally, be mindful of your creative urges right now. If you don't keep a journal, you may want to start one! Writing about your feelings, painting, or doing any other creative work could be an outlet that will keep you sane and occupied.

Give Yourself a Break

Your parents have a lot on their minds right now. Chances are, creating fun for you is not at the top of

Write about your
feelings in a journal.

their list of priorities. Guess what? It needs to be on the top of *your* list.

Do yourself a huge favor and write down ten things that you enjoy doing that don't involve your parents' participation. Do you live close to a movie theater? Do you in-line skate or read a lot? Whatever you enjoy doing is incredibly important when your parents are divorcing. It's a strange by-product of divorce, but in the long run, you're turning yourself into a more independent and creative person who knows yourself very well.

CHAPTER 5

The Economic Shift

Down to One Income

My mom and I were totally broke. My dad was supposed to send child support, but the check hadn't come yet, and I could tell my mom was getting pretty scared. She actually told me not to eat all the cheese after school because we could stretch it for a meal. I started to feel guilty every time I made a snack! I wasn't sure if I should call my dad, get a job, drop out of school, or what. — Rosa

A lot of the changes that occur with divorce are emotional. But another huge and immediate change is purely financial. For every family that is separating, there is a unique financial restructuring that takes place. Suddenly, there isn't one, but two households to support. This means two rents or mortgages, two stocked refrigerators, two cars, and more.

For many families, this is a difficult adjustment. There simply isn't the money there used to be. This may mean having to get a part-time job after school, and becoming conscious of your family's budget for the first time. But whatever you do, don't drop out of school! If you really believe it has come to that, discuss this with your school guidance counselor. They'll do everything they can to help you figure out a way to meet your obligations without allowing your education to suffer.

Types of Legal Support

There are some forms of legal support that are in place to help your family make the financial adjustments that occur with a divorce. The following are a couple of terms that you might be hearing right now.

Child Support

Child support is a monthly payment made by the parent who does not live with the child. This is a legal arrangement that is designed to help the supporting parent meet the children's needs. The law bases the amount on three factors: 1) the parents' combined income, 2) the prior lifestyle of the family, and 3) what the children's needs are.

The amount of this payment differs greatly from family to family. Some parents' payments are higher if there are tuition or medical needs to be met.

Sadly, some households have difficulty collecting these payments. Paying child support is a serious obligation that parents have after a divorce. Family courts are in place to help parents fight for their rights if the need for legal help arises.

Fortunately, laws are getting tougher. Garnishing wages (automatically deducting money from a parent's paycheck in the same way that taxes are automatically taken out) is one way family courts obtain these payments.

Spousal Support (or Alimony)

A similar arrangement to child support, spousal support is a legal payment arrangement designed by our legal system to assure that a former spouse can maintain, as well as possible, his or her previous lifestyle and meet his or her needs.

Other Solutions

Helping Out at Home

If the parent you live with also works, don't underestimate the power of housework as a tool to help keep the household running smoothly. During this stressful adjustment, helping out around the house will make everyone a lot happier.

Perhaps you get home after school earlier than your working parent does. You can use some of this time to straighten up the house and even get a head start on dinner. Baby-sitting younger siblings and mowing the lawn are other ways you could help out and even save your parent some money. Everybody's energy is precious right now, and a clean house might be exactly what your family needs.

If you have siblings who are old enough to help you out, take charge and parcel out chores in a way that is fair. Alternate so that you don't get too bored being responsible for the same things; for example, one of you can vacuum while the other washes the dishes.

Getting a Part-time Job

Getting a part-time job is a terrific way to help your household out financially. Before you do this, have a talk with your custodial parent about what contributions he or she thinks would be fair so that you won't be surprised after you bring home your first paycheck.

Have some ideas of your own to contribute to this conversation. For example, maybe you like picking out

You can help your family by getting a part-time job.

Other Budgeting Strategies (That Can Even Be Fun)

* Shop for clothes and books at your neighborhood thrift stores.
* Help your parent clip and organize coupons from newspapers (you can double the worth of these at many grocery stores).
* Find out where you can use a student ID for reduced fares to cultural events (many museums let students in for free).
* Rediscover your library for free and fun workshops, movie rentals, and even reduced-fee tutoring.

your own clothes when you go shopping. Picking up the tab for your wardrobe is a way for you to help out and to become more independent. Another way you can pitch in is with your school expenses: books, uniforms, and other fees that come up through the academic year. Even taking a bite out of your allowance could help your parent to manage your newly reduced household budget better.

Think about your location, your access to public transportation, and your homework load before you consider where to look for a job. If you simply have too much homework to consider working during the year,

Shopping in thrift stores is a cool way to save money.

get a jump on researching summer jobs, such as camp counselor. All of these elements need to be factored into your choice. Finally, think about what you enjoy doing. Do you like hanging out at the mall with your friends after school? Why not try approaching some of your favorite stores to see if they could use your help for a few hours a week?

Here are some other places you could look: your local library, restaurants and coffee shops in your neighborhood, neighbors who have young children and may need baby-sitters, hardware stores, or bookstores. Use your imagination!

Other Benefits of Working Part-time

Aside from making some extra pocket money, working part-time has lots of other benefits. It looks great on your resumé when you are applying to colleges, and many colleges would favor someone who can get a written recommendation from a boss. It's one way to prove to people how responsible you are.

Your part-time job could introduce you to new friends, teach you many skills, get you out of the house during a difficult time, and just be a lot of fun.

A part-time job looks great on college applications.

CHAPTER 6

Remarriage, Stepparents and Stepsiblings

I remember when my dad told me he was going to get remarried. He and my mom had only been divorced for two years! Plus, I didn't even know his girlfriend that well. She had two little kids! Does this mean I had to act like a big sister to them? What about my mom's feelings? — Mona

When a Parent Remarries

Once the dust settles after a divorce, your parents will be getting on with their lives. They may start dating, and yes, many will remarry. When they do remarry, the "binuclear" family takes shape. This means that where there was once one family and one household, there are now two.

As with so many other aspects of divorce, the results of this vary from family to family. Some parents may "inherit" stepchildren if they marry someone else who already has children. For the "original" children, this is very difficult. Suddenly you may feel jealous and angry about your growing family.

Just remember that for a short while families are reorganizing themselves. After years go by and your parents are with other people (hard to imagine) it may be strange for you to visualize how life was before the divorce. For a ton of parents who get divorced and remarry, marriage feels more natural and happy for them the second time around.

After the dust settles, you might be surprised. Some kids actually enjoy the change of pace of going back and forth between one place and another. It gives them a chance to enjoy two different lifestyles.

Stepsiblings and, Yes, New Babies

If you have siblings already, you know how intense these relationships can be. You either get along really well, or you fight like cats and dogs. Maybe you fall somewhere in between. Whatever your relationship is to them, one thing is for sure: You see them a lot.

Inheriting new brothers and sisters when a parent remarries is a bizarre situation. Even more confusing than inherited siblings are the children that your parent might have with his or her new spouse. If you don't live with the "new" family during the week, you may have to spend weekends with them. It can be confusing and painful to see your stepsiblings establishing a relationship with your parent. It's also weird to see your parent cooing over a new baby. After all, you came first, and it's hard to believe that there is enough attention to go around.

At first, there might not be. Your parents are adjusting to a new life, and it is probably pretty hard for them to try to juggle everything and everyone. Just as you are having a tough time with the changes, your stepparents' children are probably having an equally tough time. There is sure to be some tension somewhere, and to get through all this, it's helpful to remember a couple of things.

You did come first, and your parents love the special relationship that they have with you and you alone. No one can replace the position you have in their hearts. You might be surprised and find yourself liking things about your stepsiblings.

Try to be open to new relationships—and give yourself a break! It's natural to feel jealous, confused, and upset about all of this. After some time passes, you will have a different perspective on what these new fixtures in your life can mean to you. Besides, it may be nice to see your parent happy again.

Stepparents—Friends or Foes?

Traveling from place to place before your parent remarried was hard enough. Now, with this new parental force, it may feel awkward. One difficult thing about stepparents is certain to crop up: Suddenly you have to adhere to a new set of rules—theirs. Every parent has a unique philosophy about how to raise his or her children, and that includes your new stepparents. If they express their views about your behavior or about anything else, you may feel like they're overstepping your boundaries. If this is the case, the best thing you can do is to keep the lines of communication open between you and your "real" parent. By doing this, you prove that you are willing to give your stepparent a chance, but you need to talk about how it's affecting you.

Help keep your parents close to you instead of pushing them away. Your real parents are prepared for some conflict, hurt, and confusion in their children when they remarry. If you talk openly with them, you'll also be giving them the opportunity to discuss their feelings with you.

When Only One Parent Remarries

When I went to visit my dad and his new wife this week-end, we actually had a pretty good time. They took me to the movies, and we did some shopping. But when I came home to my mom, I felt totally guilty about the clothes Susan, my stepmom, had bought for me because my mom can't afford to shop for me right now. So I hid the clothes, and told her that I couldn't stand Susan, that she was ugly and mean to us. Now I feel guilty because I feel that I lie all the time, and that my mom will get angry at me if I tell her I actually kind of like Susan. — Sly

If you live with a parent who hasn't remarried while the other one has, you're bound to feel some loyalty toward your single parent. Your single parent is only human, and your other parent's remarriage will be difficult to adjust to, even if that period of adjustment is only temporary. If you felt a tug-of-war scenario when you were going back and forth before the remarriage, be prepared for the guilt to increase.

One natural reaction that kids have when they're going home to their single parent is to badmouth their stepparent to their single parent, so the single parent will feel better. You might be coming home to a whole new third-degree line of questioning about your mother or father's "new lifestyle." Sometimes it seems

A divorce often feels like a tug-of-war.

easier to go along with your upset parent's feelings, but at what cost? The longer this goes on, the worse you will feel. Your parent needs to be the grown-up and accept that you are building a relationship with a new stepparent. If the third-degree continues to await you every time you come home, stand your ground and tell your parent how lousy it makes you feel. Eventually, your mom or dad will hear you, and you won't have to feel bad when you come home anymore.

When divorce happens, there will be both ups and downs for a long, long time. But trust in the power of time, and tap into the strength you have inside yourself, and you'll get through it. Nothing can erase the bond you have with your family members. And as *all* of your lives change, you can make sure that these bonds always stay strong.

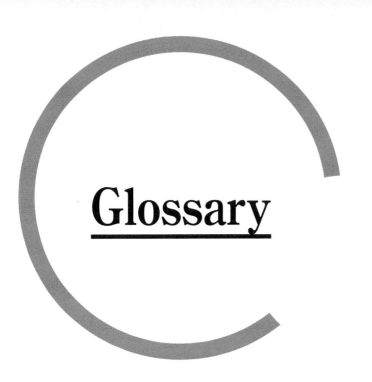

Glossary

binuclear family   Term that describes the process of both parents remarrying: Where there was once one family and one household, there are now two.

child support   A monthly payment made by the parent who does not live with the child. This is a legal arrangement that is designed to help the supporting parent meet his or her children's needs.

custody   Custody establishes with which parent a child or children will live after a divorce. Some parents divide custody, which means that the children divide their time between both parents. This arrangement is known as "joint custody."

family court   A legal system that is set up to fairly process all legal matters having to do with divorce, such as child support payments, custody, and other legal issues that arise in families.

spousal support (or alimony)   Similar to child support, spousal support is a legal payment arrangement designed to assure that a former spouse can maintain, as well as possible, his or her previous lifestyle.

Where to Go for Help

Al-Anon Family Group Headquarters, Inc.

1600 Corporate Landing Parkway

Virginia Beach, VA 23456

(800) 344-2666

Web site: http://www.al-anon.org/

This site can link you to local Al-Anon meetings—a great place to go for help if you live with an alcoholic parent or stepparent.

Banana Splits Support Group

(212) 262-4562

A school/parent support program for children of divorce, Banana Splits have meetings with many activities; role playing and peer counseling are just two examples. This program has been used by school counselors throughout the United States for many years and has been honored on major network news shows.

Childhelp
(800) 422-4453

Hotline for young people in crisis.

Children's Rights Council
300 I Street NE

Suite 401

Washington, DC 20002

(202) 547-6227

Web site: http://www.vix.com/crc/

Covenant House Nineline
(800) 999-9999

Divorcing.com
Web site: http://www.divorcing.com

A thorough on-line resource with links to a variety of subjects including the emotional, financial, and parenting issues that go along with divorce. This excellent Web site also has a chatroom and message board.

Parents Place
Web site: http://www.parentsplace.com

A Web site that often sponsors different forums and essays for parents and teenagers who are healing from the pains of divorce.

Stepfamily Association of America, Inc.

215 Centennial Mall South, Suite 212

Lincoln, NE 68508

(800) 735-0329

Web site: http://stepfam.org/

Stepfamily Foundation, Inc.

333 West End Avenue

New York, NY 10023

(212) 877-3244

(212) 799-STEP

Fax: (212) 362-7030

Web site: http://www.stepfamily.org

For Further Reading

Blume, Judy. *It's Not the End of the World.* New York: Bantam, 1986.

Hart, Archibald. *Children and Divorce: What to Expect, How to Help*. Nashville, TN: Word Publishing, 1997.

Johnson, Linda Carlson. *Everything You Need to Know About Your Parents' Divorce.* Rev. ed. New York: Rosen Publishing Group, 1998.

Johnston, Janet R., and Carla Garrity. *Through the Eyes of the Children.* New York: Simon and Schuster, 1997.

Joselow, Beth B., and Thea Joselow. *When Divorce Hits Home: Keeping It Together When Your Family Comes Apart*. New York: Avon Books, 1996.

Schneider, Meg F., Joan Zuckerberg, and Joan Offerman-Zuckerberg. *Difficult Questions Kids Ask and Are Too Afraid to Ask—About Divorce*. New York: Simon and Schuster, 1996.

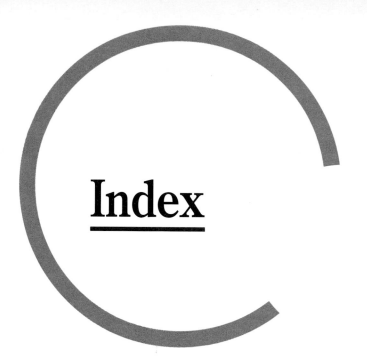

Index

Acknowledgments

I would like to acknowledge with love my brother Christian for his generosity in sharing his studio with me throughout this project, and for his ever-present love, support, and sunshine. I'd also like to thank Jim Burton for giving me the strength, safety, and love to tackle this emotional project. Finally, thanks to the New York Public Library System.

About the Author

Rachel Aydt has worked in magazines and book publishing for seven years in New York City. This is her first nonfiction book. She has published multiple magazine articles and two chap-books of poetry: one with Boog Literature, the other with 50 Gallons of Diesel Press.

Photo Credits

Cover and pp. 14, 24, 28, 31, 35, 36, 43, 45, 46 by Thaddeus Harden; p.9 by Ira Fox; p.4 by Steve Skjold; p. 33 © Index Stock; p. 52 © Corbis

Design and Layout

Michael J. Caroleo

Series Editor

Erica Smith